W9-DHU-561

THE STORY OF
BAUCIS AND PHILEMON

Pamela Espeland
pictures by George Overlie

Unity School Library
Unity Village, Missouri 64065
DISCARD

Carolrhoda Books, Inc., Minneapolis

9-87

Copyright © 1981 by CAROLRHODA BOOKS, INC.

All rights reserved. International copyright secured.
Manufactured in the United States of America

LIBRARY OF CONGRESS CATALOGING IN PUBLICATION DATA

Espeland, Pamela, 1951-
    The story of Baucis and Philemon.

    (A Myth for modern children)
    SUMMARY: An old, impoverished couple are the only
ones in Phrygia to take pity on two tired, hungry travelers
who turn out to be Jupiter and Mercury in disguise.

    1. Baucis and Philemon (Greek mythology)—Juvenile
literature. [1. Baucis and Philemon (Greek mythology)
2. Mythology, Greek] I. Overlie, George. II. Title.

BL820.B28E84   292'.13   80-27674
ISBN 0-87614-140-8

     2 3 4 5 6 7 8 9 10 92 91 90 89 88 87 86 85 84 83 82

c. 1

to David Porter, who loves what he teaches

ABOUT THIS STORY

Ancient Greece wasn't very big, but it was very important. All together, the Greek states made up an area about the size of Austria. From this tiny part of the world came many famous people and ideas.

The ancient Greek people were a lot like us. Over 2,000 years ago, their children played and went to school and watched the Olympic games. Grown-ups worked. They wrote plays and poems. They made laws. Their government was the beginning of Western democracy.

But the Greeks didn't know as much as we do about science. So they used myths to explain nature. When there was a storm at sea, they said, "Poseidon, the God of the Sea, must be angry!" When there was a good harvest, they said, "Demeter, the Goddess of the Earth, must be happy!" Not all myths explained nature, though. Some told about Greek history. And some were just good stories.

The Greek civilization lasted for a long time, but it could not last forever. Around 150 B.C., the Romans took it over. They also adopted the Greek gods and goddesses—they just changed their names to Roman names. (In this story all the names are Roman.) Most Romans didn't really believe in the gods, but they did like to tell good stories. So they kept on telling the myths.

■ Ancient Greece and her colonies shown on a modern map
⋯⋯ Modern-day Greece

The story of Baucis and Philemon was first written down by a Roman poet named Ovid. Ovid's most famous book is called *Metamorphoses*. The word "metamorphoses" means changes. Each of the poems in the book tells a story about some kind of change. There are a lot of changes in the story of Baucis and Philemon. Something happens to a town. Something happens to a little hut. And something happens to two old people.

Long ago there really was a kingdom called Phrygia. It was located in part of the country we call Turkey. Maybe two old people named Baucis and Philemon really did live there once. No one knows for sure.

"It's hard work being the King of the Gods," Jupiter said to himself one day. "I need a vacation!"

He sat on his throne and thought for a few minutes.

"Maybe I'll go down to the earth for a while. I'll ask my son Mercury if he wants to go along. We'll dress up in old clothes so people won't know we are gods. That should be fun!"

Jupiter found Mercury and told him his plan. The two gods started getting ready right away.

Mercury was the Messenger God. He carried news back and forth between all the other gods. He had wings on his feet so he could run very fast. Now he found a pair of shoes. He put them on to hide his wings. Then he covered up his beautiful robe with an old one. Jupiter put on an old robe too.

Jupiter looked at his son and smiled. "Just be sure to keep your wings tucked in," he said. "I don't want anyone to guess who we really are!"

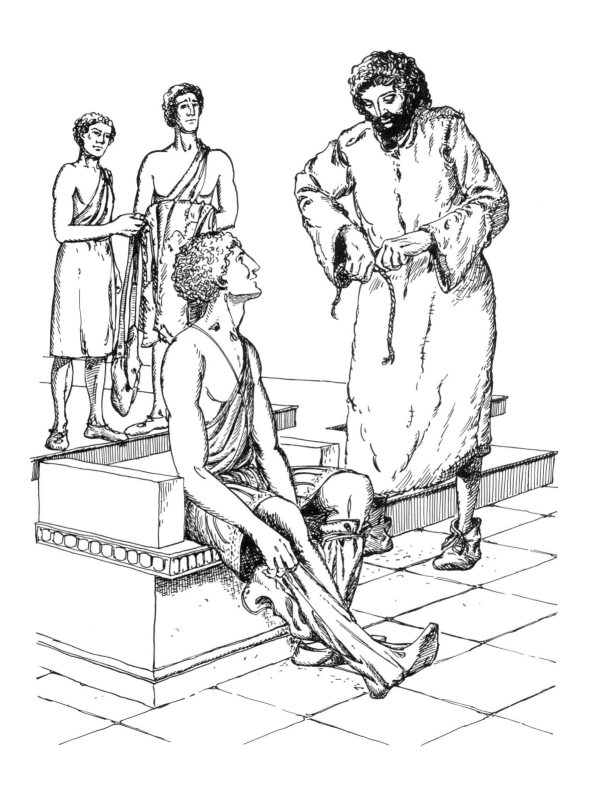

Jupiter and Mercury left their home on Mount Olympus. They went to a land called Phrygia. Soon they came to a town.

"Let's give the people who live here a test," Jupiter said. "Let's pretend we're tired, hungry travelers. We'll see if the people in this town are kind to poor strangers."

The two gods walked up to a house. They knocked on the door. A woman opened it a crack and peeked out at them.

"What do *you* want?" she asked.

"We have been traveling for many days," Jupiter lied. "We are very tired and hungry. Could you spare us a bite to eat?"

"My feet are sore," Mercury added. "Do you have someplace where we can rest?"

The woman frowned. "Why should I help you?" she asked. "I don't even know who you are. You look like a couple of bums. Go away!" Then she slammed the door in their faces.

Jupiter and Mercury walked to the next house. This time a man came to the door.

"We have been traveling for many days," Jupiter began.

But the man didn't even let the god finish talking. "Don't bother me!" he said. "I have work to do!" Then he closed his door and locked it tight.

The two gods went to house after house. But no one would let them in. No one would give them food. They went to 1,000 houses, and 1,000 people turned them away. It was getting late, and Jupiter was not having fun after all. Instead, he was very angry.

Finally Jupiter and Mercury reached the end of the town. There was only one house left. It stood at the bottom of a hill. It was just a little hut with a straw roof. It didn't even have a real door.

Inside the hut lived an old woman named Baucis and her husband, Philemon. They had lived there for many, many years, ever since they were first married. They had been poor all their lives. But they didn't mind. They were happy just being together.

Baucis was very surprised to see two strangers standing in the doorway.

"There are two poor travelers outside!" she told Philemon. "Ask them to come in! They must be tired and hungry."

Philemon walked over to the gods.

"Won't you come inside?" he asked politely. "We don't have much. But we'll be glad to share what we have with you."

Jupiter and Mercury had to bend over to walk through the doorway. Inside was a tiny room. It didn't have much furniture, but it was clean and neat.

Baucis and Philemon got busy. They did all they could to make the strangers feel at home. Philemon brought out a mattress made of grass. He put it on an old couch made of willow branches. Then he covered it with a cloth full of patches.

"Please make yourselves comfortable," he said. "Supper will be ready soon."

Baucis went to the fire and stirred the ashes. She threw in some leaves and bark and blew on them. Soon the fire was burning brightly again. Then Baucis hung a copper pot over the fire and filled it with water. Meanwhile Philemon went to the garden and got a cabbage.

There was a piece of ham hanging from a hook. The two old people had been eating it a little at a time so it would last. But now Philemon took down the ham. He cut off a big slice. Baucis put it into the boiling water with the cabbage. Together they would make a good stew.

When Baucis was setting the table, she saw that it wobbled. One leg was too short. She put a broken plate under the leg. Now the table didn't wobble anymore. She rubbed it with fresh mint so it would smell good. Then she went to a cupboard and got out all the food that was there. She brought olives, cherries, cheese, and eggs to the table. Philemon found a bottle of wine. It was the only one they had. He poured it into a clay bowl.

At last everything was ready. Philemon served his guests first. Then he served Baucis and himself. Everyone started eating. But in the middle of the meal something strange started happening. Whenever anyone poured wine out of the clay bowl, it filled right up again! Baucis and Philemon were very frightened. They had never seen anything like this before! Who *were* these travelers?

Baucis turned to the two gods. "I'm sorry we gave you such a poor meal!" she said. "But we have an old goose. We'll kill it so you can have more to eat."

Baucis and Philemon didn't really want to kill the goose. It was like a pet. It kept the two old people company during the day. It slept by their bed at night. But now

they tried to catch the goose. They ran around the room, waving their arms and shouting. The goose was too fast for them, though. Finally it ran over to Jupiter and hid beneath his robes. Baucis and Philemon didn't know what to do next.

Jupiter reached down to rub the goose's long neck.

"You don't have to kill it," he said. Then he and Mercury stood up together and took off their old clothes. Underneath, their beautiful robes shone so brightly that Baucis and Philemon covered their eyes.

"We're not really poor travelers," Jupiter said, smiling. "We are gods. I am Jupiter, and this is my son Mercury. Please don't be afraid of us."

Then Jupiter stopped smiling. "We came to Phrygia to see if the people here are kind to strangers," he said. "We went to all of the houses in town. No one but you let us in. No one but you gave us food. Now come with us. We want to show you something."

The two gods walked out of the little hut. They climbed up the side of the hill. Baucis and Philemon followed slowly. They were so old that they had to stop and rest a lot. But finally they reached the top.

"Turn around and look at the town," Jupiter said.
Baucis and Philemon couldn't believe their eyes. There
was a lake where the town used to be! Only their little
hut was left standing at the edge of the water.

Then something else happened. Their hut changed into a beautiful temple! The straw roof turned to gold. The dirt floor turned to smooth white stone. Carved gates grew up where the old doorway had been.

Baucis and Philemon were very frightened. But Jupiter spoke to them in a quiet voice.

"The people in the town deserved their punishment. But you deserve our thanks. We want to give you a present. Ask for anything."

The two old people didn't know what to do. So Philemon turned to Jupiter and asked, "May Baucis and I talk about this in private? It will only take a minute."

Jupiter nodded. Then Baucis and Philemon bowed their heads and whispered together. Finally they looked up at the gods again.

"We want to take care of your temple for as long as we live," Philemon said. "And since we have been so happy together, we want to die together. I do not want to die and leave Baucis all alone!"

"And I do not want to die and leave Philemon all alone either," Baucis added.

"You will have what you want," Jupiter promised. Then he and Mercury went back home to Mount Olympus.

Baucis and Philemon spent many years taking care of the beautiful temple. One afternoon, when they were very, very old, they went for a walk. They held hands and talked about the many years they had spent together. They remembered the two gods who had visited them long ago.

Suddenly Baucis felt funny. She turned to look at Philemon. Something was happening to her husband! There were leaves growing out of his hands and shoulders! He was turning into a tree!

Then Baucis saw that she was growing leaves too. It was all happening so quickly! The two old people barely had time to say "Good-bye!" before bark grew over their faces.

Baucis and Philemon had gotten their wish. Neither had been left alone. Instead, they stood side by side, an oak tree and a linden tree. They grew up straight and tall in front of the temple. Maybe they are still standing there today. And maybe the gods are still giving good people what they ask for.

PRONUNCIATION GUIDE

Baucis: BAW-siss
Demeter: de-MEE-ter
Jupiter: JOO-pih-ter
Mercury: MER-kew-ree
Metamorphoses: met-uh-MORE-fuh-seez
Olympus: oh-LIM-puss
Ovid: OV-id
Philemon: fih-LEE-mun
Phrygia: FRIJ-ee-yuh
Poseidon: poe-SIE-dun